In a Pickle

Chutneys • Preserves • Salsas • Sweet Treats

JILL BREWIS

photography by Karen Ellis

PENGUIN BOOKS
Published by the Penguin Group
Penguin Group (NZ), 67 Apollo Drive, Mairangi Bay,
Auckland 0632, New Zealand
(a division of Pearson New Zealand Ltd)
Penguin Group (USA) Inc., 375 Hudson Street,
New York, New York 10014, USA
Penguin Group (Canada), 90 Eglinton Avenue East,
Suite 700, Toronto, Ontario, M4P 2Y3, Canada
(a division of Pearson Penguin Canada Inc.)
Penguin Books Ltd, 80 Strand, London,
WC2R 0RL, England
Penguin Ireland, 25 St Stephen's Green, Dublin 2,
Ireland (a division of Penguin Books Ltd)
Penguin Group (Australia), 250 Camberwell Road,
Camberwell, Victoria 3124, Australia
(a division of Pearson Australia Group Pty Ltd)
Penguin Books India Pvt Ltd, 11, Community Centre,
Panchsheel Park, New Delhi – 110 017, India
Penguin Books (South Africa) (Pty) Ltd, 24 Sturdee
Avenue, Rosebank, Johannesburg 2196, South Africa

Penguin Books Ltd, Registered Offices:
80 Strand, London, WC2R 0RL, England

First published by Penguin Group (NZ), 2006
1 3 5 7 9 10 8 6 4 2

Conceived and packaged for Penguin Group (NZ)
by Renaissance Publishing
PO Box 36 206, Northcote, Auckland
New Zealand
rl@renaissancepublishing.co.nz

Designed by Gina Hochstein
Prepress by Image Centre Ltd
Printed by Condor Production, Hong Kong

ISBN - 13: 978 0 14 302061 5
ISBN - 10: 0 14 302061 7

A catalogue record for this book is available from
the National Library of New Zealand.

www.penguin.co.nz

Thanks to **nest**, Ponsonby, Auckland,
for providing many of the beautiful containers
and dishes feautured in this book.
www.nest.co.nz

DISCLAIMER
Although every effort has been made to ensure the
ingredients and instructions in this book are accurate,
neither the author nor the publisher can accept any
liability for any resulting injury or loss or damage to
property whether direct or consequential.

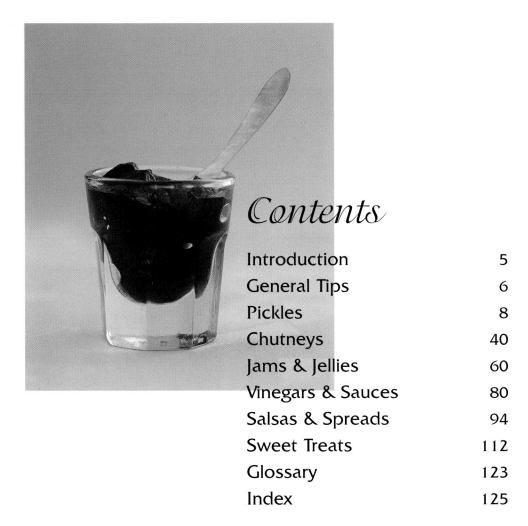

Contents

Introduction

Eat what you can, can what you can't. That was our grandmothers' dictum about preserves. When their home gardens and orchards produced more than could be used immediately, preserving surplus fruits and vegetables occupied a large chunk of their time each autumn.

Today, with many households consisting of just one or two people, the need is for small accompaniments to enhance other foods, rather than to ensure vast quantities of produce don't go to waste. Bottling, a time-intensive method of preserving surplus fruit and vegetables has, fortunately, been superseded by freezing.

Most of the recipes here for pickles, chutneys, sauces and salsas have been adapted to make smaller quantities that can be consumed within a reasonable time. After all, no one wants a fridge full of half-empty jars of relishes.

This collection includes some classic and nostalgic recipes, and some using fashionable ingredients such as balsamic vinegar and flavoured oils. All are seasonal, sensational, and yes, even sexy! (Try the Fig, Walnut and Whisky Chutney if you're a doubter.)

General Tips

Cleaning hands

If your hands and fingernails are stained from peeling fruit and vegetables, rub them with a cut lemon before washing in warm water. The lemon juice, pulp and pith remove the worst stains, even those from beetroot, berries, apples and feijoas.

Ingredients

Malt vinegar is great for pickles where its dark colour is not a distraction – with red cabbage, beetroot or pickled walnuts. White wine vinegar or good-quality white vinegar gives a superior result with light-coloured fruits and vegetables, such as garlic, apricots and beans.

Remove any soft spots or bruised areas from fruits and vegetables before using. Spices used in pickles and chutneys are best kept whole. Tie them in a small piece of muslin or fine clean cloth (a square of Chux cloth works well) to make it easy to remove and discard when pickle is cooked.

Packing into jars

Bubbles in the jar? When filling jars with hot jams, jellies, sauces or pickles, keep a metal or bamboo skewer on hand. Run it down the inside of the jar to release any visible air bubbles.

Sterilising jars

OVEN METHOD: Wash jars and stand them in an oven preheated to 150°C for 20 minutes. Keep warm until required.

MICROWAVE METHOD: Wash jars and put them, two at a time, still damp, in a microwave oven at 65 percent power. Microwave for 2 minutes.

Storage
Pickles, chutneys, sauces and vinegars should be stored in a cool, dry place. The lowest shelf of a pantry or cupboard is ideal.

Testing a jam
To test a jam or jelly for setting point, place a teaspoonful on a saucer and run a finger through it. If the two parts do not run together, it is ready.

If you don't have a jelly bag, layers of cheesecloth spread inside a sieve make a good substitute.

Utensils
Stainless steel or glass bowls and utensils are best, as these do not react to acidic ingredients such as vinegar. A traditional preserving pan, usually made of aluminium, has a top wider than its base so liquids can be boiled off.

Pickles

Courgette Strips

This method can also be used for cucumber, producing long slices ideal for use in sandwiches.

500g (about 4 medium)
    courgettes of uniform
    length
2 tablespoons salt
2 cups white wine vinegar
2 tablespoons sugar
1/2 teaspoon white pepper
1 teaspoon salt
bunch of fresh basil or mint

Trim ends from courgettes and slice thinly lengthways. Lie in a colander or sieve and sprinkle salt over courgettes. Leave for at least 2 hours.

Prepare pickling liquid by heating together vinegar, sugar, pepper, salt and herbs.

Place courgette slices on end in a warm sterilised jar, and pour in enough pickling liquid to cover them well.

Makes 1 x 500ml jar. Ready to eat in 1 week.

Pickled Courgette Salad:
Chop courgette slices into 5cm lengths. Just before serving, mix in 1 cup natural unsweetened yoghurt, 2 tablespoons chopped mint and 2 cloves minced garlic.

Acar

'You must include acar!' said my Singapore Chinese sister-in-law. Acar is the vegetable pickle that appears as a side dish whenever curry, rice, vegetables or noodles are served in Singapore.

SPICE PASTE
6 dried red chillies
1/2 medium onion, finely chopped
2.5cm piece root ginger
1 teaspoon ground turmeric
2 macadamia nuts
1 teaspoon fish sauce
2 tablespoons sesame oil

2 short cucumbers
1 large carrot
10 shallots
6 cloves garlic
4cm piece root ginger
3 red chillies
4 tablespoons sesame oil
3 teaspoons sugar
1/2 teaspoon salt
3 tablespoons white vinegar

To make spice paste, chop all dry ingredients and put in a blender with fish sauce and sesame oil. Combine until it becomes a rough paste. Set aside.

Wipe cucumbers and, without peeling, cut in half and discard seeds. Cut cucumbers and carrot into thin strips about 5cm long. In separate bowls, cover cucumber with salted water and carrot with cold water, and leave to soak.

Peel shallots and chop roughly. Crush garlic lightly and remove the skins. Peel and finely chop root ginger. Cut a slit in each chilli, removing seeds if a mild pickle is required.

Heat the sesame oil in a 30cm frying pan and fry the spice paste gently for 2–3 minutes to release the aroma. Add shallots, garlic, ginger and sugar and fry gently for a few more minutes. Stir in salt and vinegar.

Drain cucumbers and carrots and toss into the pan along with chillies. Cook over a low heat until carrot begins to soften, about 8–10 minutes, stirring occasionally to cover vegetables with sauce. Allow to cool.

Make 1 x 500ml jar. Keeps for 2 or more weeks in the refrigerator.

Chillied Olives

Add your own touch to a bowl of mixed olives with a coating of chilli, garlic and herbs.

500g mixed green and black
   olives
1 red chilli, thinly sliced
1 clove garlic, finely
   chopped
bunch of fresh thyme,
   oregano or parsley, finely
   chopped
1/2–2/3 cup extra virgin
   olive oil

Place olives in a small saucepan. Add all other ingredients, allowing enough oil to barely cover. Heat very gently until they are warmed through. Serve immediately.

Keeps up to 1 week in the refrigerator.

Anna's Olives

Olive lovers lucky enough to share some of my friend Anna's special dish are rewarded with plump fruit and a more intense olive flavour.

500g black Kalamata olives
1 cup red wine
$1/4$ cup extra virgin olive oil
1 red chilli, seeds removed,
   sliced (optional)

Preheat oven to 180°C. Place olives in a small saucepan and barely cover them with water. Bring to the boil and simmer for 1 minute. Drain well.

Into a small ovenproof dish, place olives, wine and olive oil. Bake for 30 minutes in the preheated oven, shaking the dish occasionally to ensure all sides of the olives are covered with the liquid. A little chilli added at the end of cooking is said to 'turn the sublime into heaven'. Allow to cool a little before eating.

Serve warm or cold. Recommended as a nibble with gin and tonic or wine of any sort.

To keep indefinitely, place olives back in their jar and cover with cooking liquid. Store in the refrigerator.

Anna's Olives served with Port Wine Cheese, see page 107

Pickled Olives

Processing green olives the traditional way involves three stages: soaking in a lye bath to remove the bitter taste, soaking in fresh water to remove the lye and soaking in brine to pickle them. Your local pharmacist should be able to supply the calcium carbonate for the lye bath.

Black olives are much easier to process than green olives. The hard part is collecting them from the tree as soon as they start to darken. Don't wait until the olives are nearly black or there will be none left — birds love them.

Processing Green Olives

LYE MIXTURE
made from 60g caustic soda,
   60g plain salt and
   30g calcium carbonate
   (lime)
2kg just-ripe unblemished
   green olives
775g plain salt
extra virgin olive oil

To make the lye mixture, first dissolve caustic soda in a little warm water in a large glass jar (the water may get quite hot). Add salt, calcium carbonate and 5 litres of water and stir until thoroughly dissolved.

Wash olives and place in a shallow plastic basin. Pour lye mixture over the olives. Place a piece of clean cloth on top of the olives and weigh down with a board to keep the fruit beneath the surface. Allow to stand for 3 days.

After 3 days, remove an olive and wash well. Taste it: if it is still bitter, continue steeping olives in the lye mixture for another 2 days.

Wash olives well, place in a clean container and cover with fresh water. Change water daily for 7 days to free the fruit from the hot taste of lye.

To obtain plump, wrinkle-free olives, brine slowly, increasing the strength of the brine over the next 9 days.

Dissolve 125g plain salt in 5 litres of water and pour over the olives. Allow to stand for 3 days in a cool place.

On the fourth day wash olives and cover with a brine made of 250g plain salt dissolved in a further 5 litres of water. Weigh down to ensure olives are submerged. Leave for 6 days.

After 6 days, wash olives and pack into jars. Cover with the final brine solution made by dissolving 400g plain salt in 5 litres of water. The olives can now be stored permanently in this strong brine. Cover the surface of each jar with a thin layer of olive oil.

Processing Black Olives

2kg fresh black olives
125g salt
3 litres water
extra virgin olive oil

Wash the olives in several changes of water. Drain and dry.

Make a brine with salt and water and heat, stirring until water boils and salt is dissolved. Dry olives, add to the pan and bring back to the boil.

Pack olives and brine into hot sterilised jars. Top with a layer of olive oil.

Green Bean Pickle

Most pickle recipes from the United States are very sweet, but this one is just right: neither too sweet nor too sharp. The beans stay crisp, too.

500kg green beans, trimmed and with strings removed
1½ tablespoons pickling spice
1 tablespoon black peppercorns
2 cups cider vinegar
⅓ cup sugar
2 teaspoons plain salt
1 bay leaf
1 large onion, chopped
1 red capsicum, cored, seeded and diced
1 clove garlic, peeled and minced
3 good sprigs of dill

Blanch beans in boiling water for 1 minute, then rinse under cold water, Drain well.

Tie pickling spice and peppercorns in a piece of muslin. Put them in a large saucepan with vinegar, sugar, salt and bay leaf. Bring to the boil, turn the heat down and simmer, uncovered, for 10 minutes. Add onion, capsicum and garlic and simmer for a further 10 minutes. Remove and discard muslin bag and bay leaf.

Pack beans upright into hot clean jars. Divide onion, capsicum and garlic evenly among jars. Place a sprig of dill in each jar. Pour in hot pickling liquid until overflowing, then quickly seal jars.

Makes 3 x 350ml jars.

Bread and Butter Pickles

The southern states of the USA bequeathed this recipe to the world. It makes a great topping for (wait for it) bread and butter, creating a perfect appetiser served with a pre-dinner drink.

about 10 medium
   cucumbers, washed,
   unpeeled and sliced
5 onions, peeled and
   finely sliced
4 green capsicums, cored,
   seeded and sliced
2 litres cold water
1 cup salt
7 cups malt vinegar
1.5kg white sugar
1 teaspoon each mustard
   seed and celery seed
1 tablespoon ground turmeric

Prepare cucumbers, onions and capsicum and place in a large non-metal bowl. Cover with cold water and salt, and let stand for 3 hours. Drain.

Combine vinegar, sugar, mustard seed, celery seed and turmeric in a large pan. Bring to the boil, then add drained vegetables. Bring back to boiling point, but do not let it boil. Pour into sterilised jars and seal. Serve chilled.

Makes 12 x 500ml jars.

Christmas Bread and Butter Pickles:
Use 3 green capsicums and 1 red capsicum to add the colours of Christmas to the pickle.

Grilled Capsicum Pickle

4 capsicums of different
   colours, cored, seeded
   and halved
1 cup white vinegar
1 teaspoon each salt and
   sugar
3 cloves garlic, peeled
sprigs of basil

Grill capsicum halves in the oven or over a gas flame until skin is charred. Place in a brown paper bag for 5 minutes.

Heat vinegar, salt, sugar and garlic together and simmer for 5 minutes.

Remove blackened skin from capsicums and cut the halves in half again. Pack into jars and pour in the vinegar, filling to the top of the jars. Add garlic cloves and a sprig of clean, dry basil to each jar. Seal.

Use in salads, as an antipasto, on bread or as a garnish.

Makes about 2 x 350ml jars. Ready in 3 days.

Pickled Limes

6 medium limes
1/4 cup natural flaky salt
6 bay leaves
1 tablespoon paprika
10 black peppercorns
2–3 teaspoons sugar
3/4–1 cup extra virgin
   olive oil

From left: Grilled Capsicum Pickle,
Pickled Red Capsicum, see page
20 and Pickled Limes

Wipe limes and cut into 1–2cm slices, discarding the thick ends and any pips. Place in a colander and sprinkle with salt. Leave overnight.

Layer lime slices into small sterilised jars, add bay leaves and sprinkle each layer with paprika and peppercorns. Add 1 teaspoon sugar to each jar. Cover with olive oil and seal. To use, chop and add to salads, mix with feta cheese or serve with a curry. Use flavoured oil in dressings or rub it over chicken before roasting.

Makes 2–3 small jars. Ready in 4 weeks.

Pickled Red Capsicum

A stunning colour, and surely just as good as the pickled peppers Peter Piper picked.

1 cup cider vinegar
1 cup water
1 cup sugar
2 teaspoons each salt and
   pickling spice
6–8 very ripe red capsicums
4 cinnamon sticks

Boil together vinegar, water, sugar, salt and pickling spice for 10 minutes. Clean and keep warm 4 x 500ml jars with screw-top airtight lids.

Wipe the capsicums, core and remove pith and seeds. Slice into 4 pieces lengthways or, if they are big, cut into eighths. Add capsicums to syrup and simmer for no more than 5 minutes.

Pack as many capsicum strips as possible into each jar, adding a length of cinnamon stick. Cover to overflowing with the spiced vinegar. Release any air bubbles by sliding a skewer down the inside of the jar. Screw on airtight lids.

Serve on an antipasto platter, in salads, with pasta or rice, or as a garnish.

Makes about 4 x 500ml jars. Ready to eat in 3 weeks — but they taste pretty good eaten straight away.

Marinated Mushrooms

This French treatment of small mushrooms makes them suitable for use as a salad, a pickle or a nibble with an aperitif.

200g button mushrooms
1/2 teaspoon salt
sprinkle of cayenne pepper
2 tablespoons lemon juice
4 tablespoons extra virgin
   olive oil
1 bay leaf
1 teaspoon dried thyme or
   several sprigs of
   fresh thyme

Wipe mushroom caps and trim stems. If they are large buttons, cut in half. Place in a small saucepan and sprinkle with salt and cayenne pepper. Pour lemon juice and oil over mushrooms, and add bay leaf and thyme.

Cover mushrooms with an oiled piece of baking paper or greaseproof paper and put on a tight lid. Simmer gently over low heat or in a slow oven for 30 minutes. When they are tender mix well, being careful to avoid breaking the mushrooms.

If they are to be eaten immediately, allow to cool. If not, pack into a hot clean jar while still hot and top with cooking liquid, including herbs from the bottom of the pan. If necessary, add more olive oil to ensure mushrooms are covered. Seal.

Serve sliced into salads, separately in their dressing, or drain for use as an antipasto.

Makes 1 cup.

Bulgarian Pickled Salad

A useful salad with warm spicy flavours that is good to serve in winter.

1 cup white vinegar
2 cups water
1 cup sugar
2 teaspoons salt
1 teaspoon pickling spice
1 each red, green, and
  yellow or orange capsicum
3 onions, peeled and finely
  sliced
3 tomatoes, skinned and
  quartered
3 cinnamon sticks

Make a spiced vinegar by boiling together vinegar, water, sugar, salt and pickling spice for at least 5 minutes. Wipe capsicums, core, and remove pith and seeds. Slice each capsicum into 4 pieces lengthways. Add the capsicums, onions and tomatoes to the syrup and simmer for no more than a minute.

Pack into hot clean jars, adding a cinnamon stick to each jar. Cover to overflowing with the syrup, then seal.

Makes about 3 x 350ml jars. Ready to eat in 3 weeks.

Spiced Plums

If you like the flavour of pickled fruit with meats, these are perfect. The plums, tangy with vinegar, retain their shape after preserving.

1kg sugar
5 cups malt vinegar
3 tablespoons ground
   cinnamon
1 tablespoon mixed spice
1 tablespoon ground allspice
2kg plums

Put sugar, vinegar and spices in a saucepan and bring to the boil. Turn down the heat and simmer for 10 minutes.

Meanwhile, wipe plums and prick each with a needle. Place into clean jars. Pour hot, spiced vinegar over the plums. Leave to stand for 3 days, then pour off vinegar and boil it again until it begins to thicken. Add plums, bring back to the boil, then immediately remove from the heat.

Pack plums into hot sterilised jars and pour in hot vinegar. Seal at once.

Makes about 4 x 500ml jars.

Piccalilli

Home-made piccalilli is a great stand-by for sandwiches, and as an accompaniment to cold meats and firm cheeses.

2kg mixed vegetables
   (cauliflower, onions, green
   beans, cucumber, etc)
1/2 cup salt
3 cups malt vinegar
3 green chillies
1 cup sugar
1 tablespoon mustard
   powder
1 tablespoon ground turmeric
3 teaspoons cornflour

Prepare vegetables: cut the cauliflower into florets, peel and chop the onions, slice the beans and cucumber into bite-sized pieces. Put in a large glass bowl and sprinkle with the salt. Leave for 24 hours. Drain vegetables and rinse well to remove salt.

Heat the vinegar with the chillies in a preserving pan or large saucepan, then add the prepared vegetables. Simmer for 15 minutes or until the vegetables are tender but still retain their shape.

Mix the sugar, mustard powder, turmeric and cornflour into a paste with a little cold vinegar. Stir into the vegetable mixture and simmer for 5 minutes. Stir in the sugar and cook for a further 5 minutes. Ladle into hot clean jars, seal and label.

Makes about 3 litres. Ready to eat in 1 week.

Pickled Gherkins

A great standby to have in the store cupboard.

1/2 cup salt
500ml boiling water
50 medium gherkins
1.5 litres white vinegar
300g sugar
1 tablespoon salt
1 teaspoon each whole
   allspice, yellow mustard
   seeds and white
   peppercorns
1/4 teaspoon each ground
   cloves and ground mace

Make a brine by dissolving salt in boiling water, adding more salt if required to make the brine strong enough to float an egg. Allow to cool.

Rub gherkins with a damp cloth to remove any rough spots. Trim off any stalks. Add gherkins to cooled brine and leave to stand overnight. The next day, drain gherkins and wipe each one dry.

Add vinegar, sugar and all spices to a saucepan and bring to the boil. Keep at boiling point for 10 minutes, then add gherkins. Bring back to the boil and boil for 2 minutes.

Pack gherkins into sterilised jars and pour in vinegar and spices. The next day, drain vinegar and spices into a pan and bring to the boil. Pour boiling-hot liquid over the gherkins in the jars until the jars overflow. Seal the jars.

Makes 2 x 750ml jars. Ready to eat in 2 weeks.

Pickled Green Chillies

This is the ubiquitous pickle found on restaurant tables all over Singapore.

10 fresh green chillies
1 cup white vinegar
$1/4$–$1/2$ cup boiling water

Wipe chillies with a clean, damp cloth. Discard stems and cut crossways into short chunks. Place in sterilised jars with screw-top lids. Combine vinegar with $1/4$ cup of boiling water and pour over the chopped chillies. Add more vinegar and water if necessary to cover (the amount required depends on the size of the chillies). Cool, then screw on lids.

Makes 1 x 200ml jar. Store in a dark place for at least 3 days before using.

Aubergine Salad

This marinated salad makes a welcome addition to a buffet table.

4 aubergines (eggplants)
4 medium onions
4 large potatoes
3 tomatoes, skinned and
   chopped
2 cloves garlic, minced
2 tablespoons chopped fresh
   fennel root
$1/2$ cup extra virgin olive oil
1 teaspoon sea salt
freshly ground black pepper

Bake aubergines, onions and potatoes in their skins in the oven until tender. Chop into cubes, discarding any tough skins, and place in a large bowl.

Combine tomatoes, garlic, fennel, olive oil and seasonings. Pour over the vegetables and leave to marinate for 2–3 days. Serve covered with chopped fresh green herbs.

Makes 3–4 cups.

Marinated Leeks

The French call this 'Poor Man's Asparagus'. It is good as an appetiser or in a salad, but it must be made with young tender leeks.

12 small leeks, not more than 2.5cm in diameter
1 large clove garlic, crushed
2 tablespoons white wine vinegar
6 tablespoons extra virgin olive oil
sea salt and freshly ground black pepper

Trim bases from leeks and remove any coarse green tops. Cut into 10cm lengths. Blanch leeks in boiling water for about 3 minutes. Rinse in cold water, drain well and place in a dish.

Mix together garlic, vinegar and oil. Season to taste with salt and pepper. Pour mixture over the leeks.

Ready to eat immediately. Keeps for 4 days.

Preserved Lemons

Lemons preserved in salt or extra virgin olive oil are an essential ingredient in Middle Eastern and North African cooking. A white film frequently forms on top; this is natural and easily washed off and it does not appear to affect the flavour of the lemons.

500g thick-skinned lemons (such as Meyer lemons)
50g plain salt (I use flaked sea salt without a free-running agent or other additives)
another 6 or more lemons, juiced

Have ready a sterilised, wide-mouthed jar with a screw-top plastic lid. Wash lemons and, with a stainless steel knife, cut lemons into quarters without cutting right through the stem end. Sprinkle salt inside each cut, using about 1 teaspoon per lemon.

Pack inside the jar, cutting lemons in half if necessary to fill the jar. Lemons will soften quickly and begin to release their juice; press them down lightly and top up the jar with freshly squeezed lemon juice. Extra lemon halves can be used to fill the jar. Screw the lid on the jar and store in a dark place.

To use, wash lemons to remove salt, scrape out the pulp and discard. Chop the peel. Add to chicken and meat dishes, salads and other foods where a mellow lemon flavour is desired.

Makes 1 x 500ml jar. Ready to use when soft, in a month.

Pickled Garlic

A delicious addition to an antipasto platter.

40 medium cloves garlic
1 cup cider vinegar
1/2 teaspoon mustard seeds
6 whole black peppercorns
1 teaspoon cassia buds
   or 1 x 8cm-long cinnamon
   stick
3 tablespoons white sugar

Peel garlic cloves, removing the stem end from each clove.

Put vinegar, mustard seeds, peppercorns, cassia buds (or cinnamon stick) and sugar in a small saucepan, bring to the boil and simmer for 5 minutes.

Add garlic and simmer for a further 5 minutes. Using a bamboo skewer, test the garlic for tenderness. When garlic is still crisp and the skewer can slide through the cloves, remove from heat.

Spoon garlic cloves into 2 small heated jars and pour in spicy vinegar to completely fill the jars. Screw the lids on tightly.

Keep for 1 month before using.

Pickled Roasted Garlic

Scrumptious! Use small whole bulbs of garlic if you can get them. They look as good as they taste.

200g garlic (about 10 small
   bulbs)
1 cup extra virgin olive oil

Preheat oven to 180°C. Separate cloves if using large bulbs of garlic. Remove stem end and peel. Place garlic in a small roasting dish, cover with a tablespoon of olive oil and roast in the preheated oven until the garlic is soft (about 20 minutes).

Remove from oven, allow to cool a little, then pack the garlic into 2 small sterilised jars.

Cover with olive oil to the brim of the jars.

Per's Salted Cucumber

Per, my daughter-in-law's father, who lives in the ancient Swedish city of Kalmar, says cucumber treated this way is a typical local dish. It adds flavour while retaining the cucumber's crisp texture and fresh taste.

1 telegraph cucumber
2 tablespoons plain salt
1 tablespoon sugar

Cut cucumber into thirds, leaving the skin on. Place in an airtight container. Mix salt and sugar together and sprinkle over the cucumber. Leave in a cool place for 24 hours, stirring after about 12 hours to ensure all the cucumber is covered with salt.

To serve, cut in slices about 5mm thick. Serve as an hors d'oeuvre with salmon or as part of a cold platter.

Pickled Kumquats

Kumquats are a small variety of citrus fruit with a fresh flavour similar to an orange. Here they are pickled, and eaten, skin and all.

1kg kumquats
1 cup malt vinegar
1¹/₂ cups sugar
1 teaspoon each crushed
    peppercorns and
    whole allspice
1 cinnamon stick
¹/₂ teaspoon cardamom
warm water
1 teaspoon salt

Prepare pickling solution first. Put vinegar, sugar and spices in a small saucepan, bring to the boil, turn down the heat and simmer for 15 minutes. Set aside and the flavours will meld as the liquid cools.

Wipe kumquats, cut in half and remove any seeds. Place in a saucepan, cover with warm water and salt, bring to the boil, turn the heat to low and simmer until kumquats are tender (about 30 minutes).

Remove kumquats from heat. Strain the pickling solution and add to kumquats and their liquid. Bring back to the boil, lower the heat and simmer slowly for a further 10 minutes.

Spoon kumquats into hot clean jars and top with the syrup.

When grilling or casseroling chicken, add pickled kumquats and kumquat liquid when chicken is nearly cooked. Garnish with more kumquats for a delicious citrus flavour.

Makes about 3 x 375ml jars. Keep for several weeks before using.

Kim Chi

Usually translated as pickled cabbage, this classic accompaniment to Korean meals is more a marinated salad than a pickle. There is no vinegar; the preserving medium is salt. Make it as hot as you like by altering the amount of fresh chilli used.

1 Chinese cabbage
1/2 cup natural flaky salt
5cm piece root ginger, finely
    grated (about 2 teaspoons)
bunch of spring onions,
    chopped (including some
    of the green ends)
2 cloves garlic, peeled and
    finely chopped
1/2 teaspoon cayenne pepper
1 tablespoon caster sugar
2 or more cups cold water

Wash cabbage, discarding stalk and any tired outer leaves. Chop roughly into pieces about 5cm square. In a large ceramic or glass bowl, place a layer of cabbage and sprinkle with a teaspoon of salt. Continue layering cabbage and salt until both are used up, ending with a good sprinkle of salt. Cover with a plate or saucer that presses on the cabbage and place a weight on top. Refrigerate for 5 days.

Sterilise a jar with a tight-fitting lid. Remove plate and weights, and drain off any liquid. The cabbage will have shrunk. Rinse under cold water to remove salt, then squeeze out any surplus water.

Add ginger, spring onions, garlic, cayenne pepper and caster sugar to cabbage and mix thoroughly. Spoon cabbage into jar and top up with cold water. Seal and refrigerate.

Makes 3 x 250ml jars. Ready to eat in 3 days.

Pickled Red Cabbage

Prepare this whenever you have time, so it's ready to add instant splash to your next pork or bacon dish.

1.5kg red cabbage, finely
shredded
2 tablespoons salt
1.2 litres malt vinegar
1 cup sugar
1 tablespoon each grated
fresh ginger, black
peppercorns and whole
cloves
1 teaspoon whole allspice
1 dried chilli

Place cabbage in a glass or ceramic dish and sprinkle with salt. Leave for 24 hours. Drain the (blue!) liquid that will have gathered around the cabbage.

Heat together vinegar, sugar, ginger, peppercorns, cloves, allspice and chilli. Allow to boil, then remove from heat. Pour spiced vinegar over drained cabbage. If not for immediate use, pack into sterilised jars and seal.

Makes about 6 cups.

Sweet Pickled Onions

A ploughman's lunch would not be complete without these crunchy treats on the side.

1 kg small pickling onions
$1/2$ cup plain salt
$1/2$ teaspoon black pepper
    corns
4 bay leaves
4 cloves
4 chillies (optional)
5 cups spiced vinegar
$1/2$ cup white sugar

Peel onions, sprinkle with salt and cover with water. Leave to stand for 24 hours.

Next day, drain onions and rinse in cold water. In a large saucepan bring about 6 cups of water to the boil. Add the onions and cook for 2 minutes. Drain onions and pack into sterilised jars. Add a few peppercorns, a bay leaf, a clove and, if liked, a chilli to each jar. Bring the spiced vinegar and sugar to the boil, then allow to cool slightly. Pour over onions and seal the jars.

Makes about 4 x 500ml jars. Ready in 1 month.

Chutneys

Beetroot Preserve

A good standby to serve with cold meats, with cream cheese on crackers and toast or as a spread on fresh grainy bread.

1kg fresh beetroot
500g onions, peeled
2 cups malt vinegar
1 tablespoon pickling spice
1 teaspoon salt
650g white sugar

Wash beetroot and grate coarsely. Chop onions into small dice. Place beetroot and onions into a saucepan and cover with vinegar. Tie pickling spice in muslin and add to pan, along with salt and sugar.

Boil together for 20–30 minutes until beetroot is cooked and mixture is thick. Discard spices and muslin. Spoon into hot clean jars.

Makes about 4 x 250ml jars.

Feijoa and Apricot Chutney

Originally from South America, feijoas have firmly established themselves in New Zealand, particularly in the North Island where they grow with abandon. Although feijoa bushes are prolific, the feijoa season is short, the fruit bruises easily and does not keep for more than 3 weeks. Combining them with dried apricots and the mellow tones of juniper berries makes an interesting sweet chutney.

1kg feijoas
1 cup dried apricots, chopped
2 large onions, peeled and finely chopped
2 cloves garlic, peeled and chopped
1 small red chilli, seeds removed, chopped
1 tablespoon black peppercorns
1 tablespoon juniper berries
1 cup white vinegar
2 cups brown sugar
1 tablespoon salt

Peel feijoas and chop roughly. Prepare apricots, onions, garlic and chilli. Tie peppercorns and juniper berries in a piece of muslin.

Place all ingredients into a large saucepan and bring slowly to the boil. Simmer gently for an hour or until thickened. Pour into hot jars and cover when cool.

Serve with lamb cutlets, or on rye bread with cheddar or camembert cheese.

Makes about 3 x 250ml jars.

Feijoa, Date and Pineapple Chutney

What do you do in April when all the feijoas fall off the tree? Make this chutney. It has a delicious combination of flavour and texture.

250g skinned (about 12 medium) whole feijoas

100g stoned dates, cut into thirds

1 onion, peeled and finely chopped

2 tablespoons grated root ginger

2 large cloves garlic, finely chopped

1–3 red chillies (according to heat required and strength of chillies), finely chopped

1 cup malt vinegar

1 tablespoon salt

10 whole cloves

1 stick cinnamon

1 cup sugar

225g tin crushed pineapple

Chop feijoas and dates and cover with vinegar while other ingredients are prepared. Pour into a large saucepan and add all other ingredients except pineapple. Bring to the boil and simmer for 10 minutes, or until onion is cooked. Add pineapple and bring back to the boil, simmering for 5 minutes or until chutney is thick. Spoon into hot sterilised jars.

Makes 4 x 250ml jars. Keep for 2 weeks before eating.

Fig, Walnut and Whisky Chutney

When Peter Gordon opened his restaurant Dine in Auckland, he made little jars of a fabulous fig and whisky chutney to give to his first customers. This version uses dried figs. As the liquid comes to the boil, the alcohol is burned off; orange juice could be used as a substitute for the whisky if preferred.

200g dried figs
1 cup whisky
100g walnut halves
3/4 cup brown sugar
1 teaspoon ground
  cinnamon
10 whole cloves
1 teaspoon finely chopped
  hot red chilli
fine strips of orange peel
1/4 cup white wine vinegar

Remove hard stems from figs and cut figs into quarters. Pour whisky over and leave to marinate for about 6 hours.

Break walnuts into quarters. Place all ingredients in a small saucepan and bring to the boil. Simmer for 30 minutes or until chutney starts to thicken. Pour into hot clean jars and seal.

Makes about 2 x 250ml jars.

Maharajah's Chutney

An old, hand-written recipe book indicates this very good traditional chutney came to New Zealand in the late 19th century, with the wives of British military who had served in India.

1kg firm peaches, stoned
   and chopped small
250g crystallised ginger,
   diced
500g onions, peeled and
   chopped
500g seedless raisins
125g glacé citrus peel
4 cloves garlic
500g brown sugar
1 tablespoon curry powder
2 teaspoons cayenne pepper
2 tablespoons salt
4 cups malt vinegar

Place the chopped peaches, ginger, onions, raisins, peel and garlic in a wide saucepan. Add sugar, curry powder, cayenne pepper and salt. Pour the vinegar into the pan and bring to the boil. Boil for 1 hour, stirring occasionally to keep the mixture from sticking to the bottom of the pan. Spoon into hot clean jars. Cover when cold.

Makes 4 x 500ml jars of rich, brown chutney.

Sweetcorn Relish

An all-time favourite, this colourful and tasty chutney has been around for so long that our grandmothers probably used a similar recipe. Some versions include chopped cabbage, celery or red chillies. Fresh sweetcorn is a bonus but if none is available, use tinned corn kernels.

3 large cobs of sweetcorn or
   1 x 410g tin corn kernels,
   drained
1 each red and green
   capsicum, cored, seeded
   and diced
1 medium onion, peeled and
   chopped
3 red chillies, minced
1 large clove garlic, minced
2 teaspoons white mustard
   seeds
600ml cider vinegar
2 cups sugar
2 tablespoons cornflour
1 tablespoon each turmeric
   and curry powder

Strip kernels from sweetcorn cobs and prepare capsicums, onion, chillies and garlic.

Place mustard seeds, vinegar and sugar in a saucepan and bring to the boil. Add corn, capsicum and onion to the pan and bring back to the boil. Simmer for 20 minutes.

Mix cornflour, turmeric and curry powder together with a little cold water and stir into the saucepan. Simmer for 10 minutes, stirring occasionally. Pour into hot sterilised jars and seal.

Makes about 3 x 500ml jars. Ready in 2 weeks (if you can wait that long).

Southern Tomato Chutney

American pickles are usually much sweeter than those from other countries. This one is adapted from a recipe from the Blue Willow Inn in Georgia, where it is served every day with local specialties such as fried green tomatoes and turnip leaves. It's surprisingly spicy and very good.

400g tin tomatoes with
  green capsicum
1 small onion, peeled and
  diced
1 large or 2 small
  courgettes, sliced very
  thinly
3/4 cup raw sugar
1/4 cup white sugar
1 teaspoon each salt and
  white pepper
200ml white vinegar

Place all ingredients into a saucepan and bring to the boil. Simmer for 1 hour or until thick and vegetables are tender.

Makes 2 x 350ml jars. Ready to eat immediately.

Chilli Jam

Regardless of the name, this is really a chutney. Serve it with well-flavoured fish such as hapuka, or with chops, steaks, ham or cheese. It's also good on a ploughman's platter, as it complements almost any savoury food.

1 teaspoon vegetable oil
1 onion, peeled and finely
  chopped
2 cloves garlic, crushed and
  chopped
2 red chillies, seeds
  removed, finely chopped
grated rind and juice of
  1 orange
1 tablespoon each honey
  and white vinegar

Heat oil and gently sauté onion for a few minutes until it begins to soften. Add garlic and chillies and cook for a further 2 minutes. Stir in orange rind and juice, honey and vinegar. Simmer gently for 5 minutes.

Spoon into hot sterilised jars and seal when cold.

Makes 1 x 250ml jar.

Gingered Tomato Chutney

A fresh chutney that marries well with a myriad of dishes, from Asian to Italian.

1 cup mirrin (rice vinegar
   can be used, but if so,
   increase the brown sugar
   to $1/4$ cup)
2 tablespoons brown sugar
1 tablespoon minced root
   ginger
500g ripe tomatoes, skinned
   and diced
1 cinnamon stick

In a small saucepan combine mirrin, sugar and ginger. Keep at a medium heat until sugar dissolves. Add tomatoes and juice, and cinnamon stick. Bring to the boil and simmer, uncovered, until mixture begins to thicken, about 20 minutes. Stir occasionally. Remove cinnamon stick. Pour into clean containers and cover.

Serve at room temperature with eggs, fish, fish cakes or Thai curries.

Makes $1^1/2$ cups.

Rhubarb Chutney

This recipe is so good that it's been passed on to friends and neighbours over several generations.

1kg rhubarb, weighed after
  trimming
500g onions, peeled and
  roughly chopped
125g dates, stoned and
  chopped
300ml water
300ml malt vinegar
500g brown sugar
1 teaspoon each ground
  ginger and salt
1/2 teaspoon cayenne pepper

Wash rhubarb and remove any strings, then cut into 5cm lengths.

Place all ingredients in a wide saucepan and bring to the boil over a low heat. Turn down the heat and allow to simmer, stirring occasionally, for 20 minutes or until it begins to thicken. Pour into hot sterilised jars and cover when cold.

Makes about 5 x 500ml jars.

Parsnip and Orange Chutney

Dark and delicious, this is a rich and fruity treat that even non-parsnip lovers enjoy. It is one of the few chutneys cooked with a lid on the saucepan. Usually it is necessary to leave the pan open to allow the steam to escape and liquid to concentrate; here, covering the pan allows the parsnip to cook until tender without the other ingredients drying out.

500g parsnips, peeled and diced

2 large onions, peeled and diced

rind of 1 orange, finely pared and cut into strips

2 oranges, peeled and chopped

1/2 cup dates, stoned and chopped

1 large apple, peeled, cored and diced

1 teaspoon mustard seeds

2 teaspoons pickling spice, including 2–3 chillies

1 cup sultanas

1 cup sugar

2 teaspoons ground ginger

2 cups cider vinegar

Prepare parsnips, onions, orange rind and flesh, dates and apple. Tie mustard seeds and pickling spice in a muslin cloth.

Place all ingredients in a wide saucepan and bring to the boil. Cover the pan and boil for 1^{1}/2 hours. Cool, spoon into hot sterilised jars and seal.

Serve with grilled meats and chicken, sausages and ham. It's a great complement to cheddar cheese on a ploughman's platter.

Makes 3 x 350ml jars. Ready to eat now, but keeping it intensifies the flavour.

Parsnip and Orange Chutney and Ritz Chutney, see page 54

Ritz Chutney

My mother-in-law's recipe for Ritz Chutney was famous and shared with everyone who admired the dark, spicy brew it produced. It requires a pie melon, which is not often found in fruit shops. Ask your greengrocer to source one for you.

6kg pie melon
2 tablespoons dried whole
  red chillies
500g dates, stoned
250g garlic, peeled
500g sultanas
4kg sugar
100g plain salt
1.8 litres malt vinegar

Peel skin from pie melon, discard seeds and chop flesh into 2cm cubes. Finely chop chillies, dates and garlic. Mix all ingredients together in a large saucepan and leave to stand overnight.

Next day bring chutney mixture to the boil and cook gently, uncovered, for 2 hours or until golden brown. Pour into hot sterilised jars and seal. The chutney will be runny at first, but will soon thicken.

Makes up to 10 x 500ml jars. Ready after 3 months.

Plum Chutney

4kg dark plums
2 cups raisins
2 cups sultanas
4 cloves garlic, peeled and
  crushed
7 cups brown sugar
2 teaspoons each mixed spice
  and ground pepper
3 teaspoons salt
7 cups malt vinegar

Wash plums and remove stalks. Place all ingredients in a large saucepan. Bring to the boil and continue boiling, stirring often, for about $2^1/_2$ hours. As the chutney cooks, skim out the stones with a slotted spoon. Pour into hot sterilised jars, cover and label.

Makes about 8 x 500ml. Keeps indefinitely.

Pineapple Chutney

1 x 440g tin crushed pineapple
100g sultanas
1 onion, peeled and finely
  chopped
2 tablespoons grated root
  ginger
2 cloves garlic, peeled and
  finely chopped
1 red chilli, finely chopped
1 cup malt vinegar
10 whole cloves
1 cinnamon stick
1 cup sugar

Place all ingredients in a saucepan and bring to the boil. Stirring occasionally to prevent it sticking, simmer for 10 minutes or until onion is cooked through and chutney begins to thicken. Remove cinnamon stick. Pour into hot sterilised jars.

Makes about 3 x 350ml jars. Can be used immediately, or keep for 2 weeks to allow the flavour to intensify.

Banana and Peanut Chutney

This concoction is ideal with chicken or lamb curries.

3 bananas, mashed

3 medium onions, peeled
   and diced

1/2 cup stoned dates,
   chopped

1 cup vinegar

1 cup water

1/2 cup sultanas

1/4 cup crystallised ginger,
   chopped

1/2 teaspoon each salt and
   curry powder

1/2 cup peanuts

1/2 cup sugar

Mash bananas, taking care not to make them too mushy. In a preserving pan or large saucepan, place bananas, onions, dates, vinegar and water. Bring to the boil, lower heat and simmer, stirring occasionally, for 15–20 minutes until the onion is tender. Add sultanas, ginger, salt, curry powder, peanuts and sugar. Bring to the boil, then simmer gently for 1 hour. Spoon into hot sterilised jars and cover.

Makes 3 medium jars.

Pear and Ginger Chutney

Hard pears from an ancient tree were successfully used to make this well-spiced chutney.

4 cups peeled and chopped
  pears (1.5kg)
2 medium onions, peeled
  and sliced
$1/4$ cup sugar
$1/4$ cup seedless raisins
1 cup chopped crystallised
  ginger
$1/2$ cup cider vinegar
salt
$1/4$ teaspoon cinnamon
$1/8$ teaspoon each allspice
  and ground cloves
1 clove garlic, finely chopped

Prepare pears and onions. Place in a large saucepan and add all other ingredients. Simmer gently for half an hour or until pears are tender, stirring frequently to prevent sticking. Pour into hot sterilised jars.

Makes about 3 x 350ml jars.

Rose Onion Chutney

3 red onions, peeled and
    finely cut into rings
1/4 cup sugar
300ml balsamic vinegar
1 fresh chilli, finely chopped
    (optional)

Place onions, sugar and balsamic vinegar in a saucepan and heat gently until boiling. Add chilli if a hot chutney is required. Lower the heat and, stirring occasionally, cook for 15–25 minutes until the mixture becomes thick and sticky. Pour into a hot sterilised jar.

Serve with barbecued meat, steaks, sauces or chicken. Any chutney not used immediately can be stored in the fridge in an airtight jar for 2 weeks.

Makes 1 x 350ml jar.

Tamarillo Chutney

1.5kg tamarillos, peeled and
    chopped
500g onions, peeled and
    finely sliced
250g apples, peeled, cored
    and chopped
600ml malt vinegar
750g brown sugar
1 tablespoon salt
1/2 teaspoon cayenne pepper
1 teaspoon mixed spice

Prepare tamarillos, onions and apples, and place with all other ingredients in a large saucepan. Bring to the boil, turn down the heat and simmer gently for 1 1/2 hours, stirring often. Pour into hot sterilised jars and seal.

Makes about 4 x 500ml jars.

Jams & Jellies

Lemon Honey

How do you like to eat lemon honey? On scones? On toast? It's so good you can also eat it by itself with a spoon. This recipe is from an 1850s cookbook, where it is described as 'lemon for tartlets that will keep for a year'. Call it lemon honey, lemon curd, lemon cheese or lemon jam; this is a very good version.

grated rind and juice of
   2 big juicy lemons
2 eggs
1 cup white sugar
30g butter

Prepare lemons.

Place all ingredients in a saucepan. Beat with a fork to combine. Place over a low heat and stir carefully as it cooks and thickens. Pour immediately into hot sterilised jars.

Makes 2 x 250ml jars. Best used within 2 weeks.

Best Berry Jam

This recipe comes from Sweden, land of lakes, pine forests and lovely preserves.

250g blueberries
1 cup caster sugar
2/3 cup water
2 tablespoons lemon juice
4 cinnamon sticks

Pick over the berries and remove their 'tails' and any leaves or twigs.

In a small- to medium-sized saucepan, combine sugar, water and lemon juice. Stir over a low heat without boiling until sugar has dissolved completely. Add blueberries and cinnamon sticks. Bring to the boil, reduce heat, and simmer for 5 minutes, stirring occasionally.

Test for setting point (see method page 7) and if necessary, continue to simmer until setting point is reached. Pour into hot sterilised jars and seal.

This is wonderful served with lemon meringue pie, and with creamy desserts such as crème brûlée.

Makes 1 x 350ml jar.

Courgette and Ginger Jam

This is a great way to use courgettes that have grown into marrows overnight, but courgettes of any size can be used.

2kg courgettes, peeled and cubed
juice and rind of 4 lemons
6 cloves
2.5cm piece root ginger, peeled and chopped
1.5kg sugar
100g crystallised ginger, chopped

Remove seeds from marrow-sized courgettes, cube and steam until tender. Cube smaller courgettes. Place courgette cubes in a large bowl and add lemon juice and rind, cloves, ginger and sugar. Stir until well mixed, cover and leave for 24 hours.

Next day, pour into a large saucepan or preserving pan, and heat slowly until sugar is dissolved. Add crystallised ginger, increase the heat and boil until courgette is transparent and syrup is thick. Check for setting point (see method page 7) and when set, remove from heat. Ladle into warm sterilised jars, cover and store in a cool place.

Makes about 6 x 500ml jars.

Spiced Apricots with Star Anise

1.5kg apricots
2 cups each white vinegar
   and white sugar
6–8 whole star anise
1 cinnamon stick

Choose perfect apricots. Wash and remove stalks, cut in half and remove stones.

Place vinegar, sugar and spices in a 1.5 litre saucepan. Bring to the boil, stirring to dissolve sugar. Add apricots and turn down heat. Poach gently for 5 minutes or until apricots are soft but still keep their shape. Remove cinnamon stick but reserve whole star anise. Pour into 3 or 4 x 250ml sterilised jars, adding at least 1 of the reserved star anise to each jar. Serve with pork.

Plum Jam

Damsons and satsumas produce a jam with a deep burgundy colour, while yellow plums produce a deep orange-coloured jam.

2.5kg plums
2 cups cold water
1 vanilla bean
7 cups sugar

Halve plums and remove as many stones as you can. The remaining stones can be lifted out with a slotted spoon as the jam cooks.

Place plums in a preserving pan with water. Add vanilla bean. Bring to the boil, lower heat and simmer until fruit is soft. Add sugar and stir until dissolved. Bring to the boil and continue boiling until setting point is reached (see method page 7). Pour into about 5 x 350ml sterilised jars.

Spiced Rhubarb Conserve

Sweet enough to use as jam on the breakfast toast, this conserve also goes well with roast and grilled meats.

1.5kg rhubarb
1 cup malt vinegar
1 cup water
1 cinnamon stick
1/2 teaspoon each whole
    cloves, whole allspice and
    grated nutmeg
1kg sugar
200g raisins

Wash rhubarb, remove strings, then cut into 2cm lengths.

Place vinegar and water in a saucepan, add cinnamon stick and spices tied up in a muslin square. Add sugar. Bring to the boil and simmer for 15 minutes. Add rhubarb and raisins and cook gently, stirring occasionally, for about 20 minutes until the mixture thickens. Pour into sterilised jars and cover when cool.

Makes 3 x 500ml jars.

Strawberry Conserve

A thick fruit jam that, according to a friend who has used this recipe for years, always increases your feeling of wellbeing.

2kg strawberries, hulls
    removed
12 cups sugar
3 teaspoons tartaric acid

Prepare the strawberries and place in a preserving pan or wide-mouthed saucepan. Add sugar and tartaric acid. Bring to the boil, lower heat and simmer for about 1 hour. When setting point is reached (see method page 7), pour into hot sterilised jars and cover.

Makes about 6 x 350ml jars.

Quince Conserve

Quince conserve looks delightful, like a golden jelly with pieces of fruit floating inside.

2kg quinces
2 cups cold water
8 cups cold water
about 6–8 cups sugar

Wipe quinces to clean them and remove any down. Place them whole in a large saucepan or pressure cooker with first measure of water. Boil until tender (about 30 minutes in the pressure cooker, about 1 hour in a pan).

When cool enough to handle, peel and core. Place peelings in a pan, reserving the fruit. Cover peelings with second measure of water. Bring to the boil and simmer for 45 minutes. Strain into a jelly bag suspended over a bowl to catch the liquid and leave to drip overnight.

Meanwhile, dice the cooked quince, cover and store in the fridge overnight.

Next day, discard peelings in the jelly bag, measure strained juice and weigh reserved diced fruit. Allow 1 cup of sugar for each cup of juice, and 1 cup of sugar for each cup of fruit. Pour juice and fruit into a pan, bring to the boil and add both measures of sugar. Continue to boil until setting point is reached (see method page 7). Cool slightly before pouring into hot dry jars. Seal when cold.

Makes 4 x 500ml jars.

Jams & Jellies

Red Onion Jam

3 red onions, peeled and
    finely cut into rings
1/4 cup sugar
300ml balsamic vinegar
1 fresh chilli, finely chopped
    (optional)

Place onions, sugar and balsamic vinegar in a saucepan and heat gently until boiling. Add chilli if a hot chutney is required. Lower heat and, stirring occasionally, cook for 15–25 minutes until the mixture becomes thick and sticky.

Serve with barbecued meat, steaks, sauces or chicken. Any chutney not used immediately can be stored in the fridge in an airtight jar for 2 weeks.

Makes 1 cup.

Orange Whisky Marmalade

Make this in winter when New Zealand oranges are at their juiciest.

3 thick-skinned oranges
1 large lemon
1 litre water
3 cups sugar
1/4 cup whisky

Slice oranges and lemon very thinly, then cut slices into quarters. Discard all pips. Cover with water and leave to soak until the next day.

Boil up fruit and water, stirring occasionally, for 30–40 minutes or until fruit is tender. Add sugar and boil rapidly until setting point is reached (see method page 7), about 10–15 minutes. Stir in whisky and remove from heat. Pour into hot sterilised jars and cover.

Makes 2 large or 4 small jars of delicious marmalade.

Marmalade

Marmalade is easy to make. It sets more readily if made early in the grapefruit season, but even if it's made with very ripe fruit and the result is a bit runny, it is still very good. Here is the basic recipe using New Zealand's ubiquitous grapefruit.

6 large grapefruit, skins included, diced by hand or chopped in food processor

2 lemons, chopped small, pith removed

3.5 litres water

3.5kg sugar

Prepare fruit, place in a large preserving pan and cover with water. Leave to stand for 12 hours.

Bring fruit and water to the boil slowly, then boil until tender (15–20 minutes). Allow to cool, then add sugar and leave to stand for another 12 hours.

Boil up marmalade again until setting point is reached (see method page 7), about 45 minutes. Pour into hot sterilised jars and cover.

Makes about 10 x 500ml jars.

Tomato Marmalade

When staying at Arles, an old homestead operating as a bed-and-breakfast on the banks of the Whanganui River, we were served this memorable marmalade/jam for breakfast.

2kg tomatoes, skinned and
    chopped into small pieces
125g crystallised ginger,
    shredded
3 lemons
1.6kg sugar

Prepare tomatoes and crystallised ginger. Wash lemons, quarter them and slice thinly, reserving pips. Tie pips in a muslin bag.

Place tomatoes, ginger, lemon and pips in a saucepan with sugar. Add sufficient water to barely cover. Place pan over a very low heat and stir until sugar has dissolved. Bring to the boil and simmer gently for up to 2 hours until thickened and setting point is reached (see method page 7). Pour into warm clean jars. Cover and seal.

Makes about 8 x 350ml jars.

Guava Jelly

Guavas come in all shapes and sizes and even in different colours. All are suitable for use in this recipe.

1.75kg guavas
³/₄ cup water
juice of 1 lime
sugar

Wash guavas and cut in half if large. Place in a large saucepan with water and bring to the boil. Reduce heat and simmer for 30 minutes or until fruit is tender. Pour into a jelly bag and leave to drain overnight or for at least 10 hours.

Discard fruit pulp and measure juice. Return juice to the saucepan and add 1 cup of sugar for every cup of juice. Add lime juice. Bring to the boil slowly, stirring until the sugar is dissolved. Boil briskly for 10 minutes, skimming off any foam from the surface.

Test for setting point (see method page 7). When jelly is ready, pour into hot sterilised jars. Cover and store.

Makes about 3 x 350ml jars.

Grape Jelly

Grape varieties that are unsuitable for wine-making, such as Albany Surprise and Black Homburg, make a magnificent dark purple jelly.

2kg red grapes
$3/4$ cup water
juice of 1 lemon
sugar

Wash grapes (retaining any stalks) and place in a large saucepan with water. Place over a very low heat and slowly bring to the boil. Simmer gently for 30 minutes or until fruit is cooked to a pulp. Pour into a jelly bag and leave to drain overnight or for at least 10 hours.

Discard pulp and measure juice. Return juice to sauce and add 1 cup of sugar for every cup of juice. Add lemon juice. Bring to the boil, stirring until sugar is dissolved. Boil briskly for 10 minutes, skimming off any foam from the surface.

Test for setting point (see method page 7) and when set, pour into hot sterilised jars, cover and label.

Makes about 3 x 350ml jars.

Apple and Kiwifruit Jelly

1kg green apples, chopped,
  including skins and cores
4 cups water
sugar
1 cup peeled and chopped
  kiwifruit

Prepare apples and place in a preserving pan or wide saucepan. Add water until apples are just covered. Bring to the boil and simmer until apple is pulped. Strain overnight through a jelly bag or muslin cloth. Do not squeeze.

Next day, measure juice and pour into a clean pan. Discard the apple pulp. For each cup of juice, add 1 cup of sugar. Heat slowly, stirring to dissolve sugar. When sugar dissolves, bring jelly to the boil and boil rapidly until setting point is reached (see method page 7), usually 10–15 minutes, depending on the amount of pectin in the apples. Allow jelly to cool a little. Add chopped kiwifruit and stir to spread the fruit evenly through the jelly. Pour into sterilised jars and seal.

Makes 2 x 250ml jars.

From left: Grape Jelly, see page 73, Apple and Kiwifruit Jelly, and Quince Jelly, see page 77

Crabapple Jelly

Crabapples are rich in pectin and set readily into a red-orange jelly.

1kg crabapples
4 green apples, chopped
  with skin on (not cored)
1 cup water
sugar
1 strip lemon rind

Wash crabapples and place with apples, cores included, in a preserving pan. Add water and cook until fruit is pulpy. Pour into a jelly bag to strain and leave overnight.

Measure juice and place in the cleaned preserving pan. Bring to the boil, then add 1 cup of sugar for each cup of juice. Stir until dissolved, add lemon rind and boil quickly for 10 minutes. Test for setting point (see method page 7) and when ready, remove lemon rind and pour into sterilised jars.

Makes about 3 x 250ml jars.

Quince Jelly

In colour, quince jelly is like a beautiful reddish-gold coloured gemstone. For best results, make only a small quantity at a time.

3 large quinces
cold water
1 thick slice of lemon
1–1¹/₂ cups sugar

Wipe quinces clean and chop, without peeling or coring. Place in a saucepan with a solid base, cover with cold water, add lemon slice and bring slowly to the boil. Simmer for 30 minutes with the lid on the pan, then uncover and simmer until fruit is reduced to a pulp.

Pour into a jelly bag and allow to drain for 6 hours or overnight. Do not squeeze the bag or jelly could go cloudy.

Measure juice. For each cup of juice, allow 1 cup of sugar. Bring juice to the boil and add sugar, stirring to dissolve. Boil vigorously until setting point is reached (see method page 7). Pour into hot clean jars and cover with sterilised lids.

Makes about 2 x 250ml jars of golden-red jelly.

Mint Jelly

An old favourite that still presses the buttons.

1 cup mint leaves, packed
750ml white vinegar
350g white sugar
200ml hot water
6 tablespoons powdered
   gelatine
$1/2$ teaspoon salt
2 drops green food colouring

Strip mint leaves from stalks and chop finely.

In a medium saucepan bring vinegar and sugar to the boil, stirring until sugar is dissolved. Boil for 5 minutes.

Sprinkle gelatine on top of the hot water and stir until dissolved. Add gelatine, mint and salt to hot vinegar and bring back to the boil. Remove from heat immediately (this helps retain the colour of the mint). Add green colouring and leave to cool, stirring occasionally. When jelly begins to set, pour into small jars and cover.

Makes 4 x 350ml jars.

Vinegars & Sauces

Vinegars can be flavoured with herbs and spices, wine, or fruit. As soft fruits such as berries give up their flavour readily, they are ideal to use in this way.

Blueberry Vinegar

For other fruit vinegars, use cherries, peaches or strawberries instead of blueberries.

1 cup fresh blueberries • 1$^1/_2$ cups mirrin (Japanese wine vinegar)

Pick over blueberries to remove stalks and twigs. Place half the blueberries in a small saucepan with mirrin. Bring to the boil and keep at boiling point for 3 minutes. Remove from the heat and allow to cool.

Strain the blueberry-flavoured vinegar. Place remaining blueberries in a clean dry bottle and pour in the strained vinegar. The blueberries will float on the surface. Seal bottle with a cork or screw cap.

Makes 300ml.

Raspberry Vinegar, see page 82, Spiced Vinegar, see page 83, Herbed Wine Vinegar, see page 83, and Blueberry Vinegar

Raspberry Vinegar

A special treat when added to salad dressings or to sauces to serve with white fish.

1 cup fresh raspberries • 1 teaspoon honey • 1^1/$_2$ cups apple cider vinegar

Place half the raspberries in a small saucepan, add honey and vinegar and bring to the boil. Keep at boiling point for 3 minutes. Remove from the heat and leave to cool.

Strain the vinegar from the fruit. Place remaining half of raspberries in a clean dry bottle. Pour in the vinegar. Seal bottle with a cork or screw cap.

Makes 300ml.

Red Wine Vinegar

If you want to impress your friends, use an attractive bottle and design a smart label worthy of this superior vinegar.

^{2}/$_3$ cup red wine • 1 whole clove garlic, peeled and lightly crushed • 6 peppercorns •sprigs of thyme or rosemary • about ^{3}/$_4$ cup malt vinegar

Put red wine, garlic, peppercorns and herbs in a small bottle. Top with malt vinegar. Seal tightly. Leave in a light place for 3 weeks to allow the flavours to mellow.

Makes 250ml.

Herbed Wine Vinegar

An inspired way to use up the last wine in the bottle.

125ml white wine • 2–3 cloves garlic, peeled • 1 teaspoon black peppercorns • sprigs of rosemary, thyme or marjoram • 1 bay leaf • $1/2$ cup white vinegar

Place wine, garlic and seasonings in a small saucepan. Add vinegar and bring to the boil gently. Simmer for 10 minutes. Pour into a bottle with a screw top. Leave somewhere light, such as a windowsill, for 3 weeks before using.

Makes 250ml.

Spiced Vinegar

1 litre white vinegar • 1 tablespoon each black peppercorns and white mustard seeds • 1 teaspoon whole allspice • 2 bay leaves • 1 teaspoon each sliced root ginger and whole cloves • 1 cup sugar

Heat all ingredients slowly in a saucepan until boiling, stirring to dissolve sugar. Simmer for 10 minutes, then leave to cool. Strain and bottle.

Makes 1 litre.

Apricot Sauce

A good plum sauce can also be made with this recipe, simply by substituting plums for apricots.

3kg ripe apricots, stoned and quartered

750g tomatoes, skinned and quartered

1kg apples, peeled, cored and chopped

4 large cloves garlic, peeled and chopped

3 teaspoons each whole cloves and whole black peppercorns

2.5 litres vinegar

6 teaspoons salt

3 teaspoons ground ginger

2 teaspoons cayenne pepper

Prepare apricots, tomatoes, apples and garlic. Tie cloves and peppercorns in a square of muslin. Place all ingredients in a preserving pan or large saucepan. Bring to boil and simmer until pulped, about 3 hours.

Allow to cool for half an hour, then blend until smooth. Cool completely before pouring into bottles.

Makes about 4 litres.

Cranberry and Orange Sauce

Thanksgiving Day, the last Thursday in November, is an American family affair that pays homage to food and the harvest. When I visited my son-in-law's family for Thanksgiving, everyone brought their favourite food. To accompany the roast turkey, we made this tangy cranberry sauce with fresh cranberries that ranged in colour from dark red to blotchy white.

750g fresh cranberries
1 cup fresh orange juice
$1/2$ cup water
$1^1/2$ cups sugar
$1/3$ cup red wine
1 teaspoon ground
   cinnamon
5 whole cloves
grated rind of 1 orange

Place cranberries, orange juice, water, sugar, red wine, cinnamon and cloves in a saucepan and bring to the boil. Lower heat, cover and simmer for 15 minutes. Add grated orange rind. Pour into an attractive bowl and serve warm or cold.

Makes 3–4 cups. Keeps for up to 2 weeks in the refrigerator.

Plum Sauce

In the suburb where I live, this is known as Suzanne's Sensational Sauce — each year Suzanne makes several batches to give away to her friends.

3kg red plums, stalks
  removed
1.5kg sugar
2 litres malt vinegar
1¹/₂ tablespoons salt
1 tablespoon ground ginger
1 teaspoon each whole cloves
  and cayenne pepper

Place all ingredients in a preserving pan or a large saucepan and bring to the boil. Turn down the heat and simmer until mixture begins to thicken, about 2 hours. Lift out stones with a slotted spoon and strain if desired. Pour into heated bottles. Cover when cold.

Makes about 3.5 litres.

Cumberland Sauce

A classic recipe from olde England. Constance Spry records that when she complimented the maître d'hôtel of a Paris restaurant on the Cumberland sauce being served, he replied, 'Madame, the secret is two tablespoons of Grand Marnier. It makes all the difference.' Try it if you want to pamper yourself and your guests.

3 tablespoons redcurrant
  jelly
1/2 teaspoon ground ginger
1 tablespoon finely shredded
  orange or lemon rind
2 tablespoons each fresh
  lemon juice, port, and red
  wine or Grand Marnier

Melt jelly over low heat but do not bring to the boil. Remove from heat. Add remaining ingredients and stir to combine. Do not worry if the jelly is still a bit lumpy. Pour into a jar and cover tightly.

Use with ham, pork, boiled or grilled bacon, venison steaks or casseroles. It also goes well with nut loaf and lentil dishes.

Makes 1 cup.

Horseradish Sauce

There is no comparison between most commercial horseradish sauces or creams and the real thing. Fresh horseradish has a powerful aroma and taste, so pungent when grated that it can make your head feel like it's going to blow off! It's worth the runny eyes and sore sinuses to get this brilliant sauce.

200g fresh horseradish root
250ml whipped or sour
   cream
2 tablespoons white vinegar
1 teaspoon each dry
   mustard powder and salt

Scrub horseradish under cold water and, using a potato peeler, scrape off any dark skin. Chop horseradish into small pieces and place in a blender or food processor. Process until finely grated but not completely smooth.

Mix together cream, vinegar, mustard powder and salt. Stir in 150g of grated horseradish. Allow to stand for 15 minutes, then taste for flavour, adding more horseradish as necessary to make it really pungent.

Essential with hot or cold roast beef. Also good with cold chicken, mashed into sardines, or served with smoked salmon.

Makes about 12 servings. Best used within 4 weeks; freeze any unused grated horseradish until required for the next bowl of sauce.

Greek Tomato Sauce

The mother of a Greek friend gave this recipe to me — it's perfect to make in summer when tomatoes are prolific and cheap, and freeze for winter meals of pasta, pizzas, casseroles and grilled meats.

1kg large ripe tomatoes
extra virgin olive oil
2 large onions, peeled and
   thinly sliced
1 cup stock or tomato juice
1 tablespoon sugar
basil, oregano or parsley
2 cloves garlic, crushed
sea salt and freshly ground
   black pepper

Skin tomatoes and chop roughly. Heat oil and fry onions gently until golden. Add tomatoes and stock or tomato juice. Stir in sugar, herbs and garlic, and season well. Simmer for at least 20 minutes. If more liquid is needed, add 125ml (1/2 cup) of water.

To freeze, pour into containers with tight-fitting lids. Extract as much air as possible and freeze quickly.

Pan Yan Sauce

This German recipe makes a good quantity of spicy fruit sauce. Any soft fruit, including persimmons, feijoas, grapes, peaches and plums, can be used.

1.5kg fruit, cored, peeled
and chopped
500g onions, peeled and
diced
4 cloves garlic, peeled and
finely chopped
3.5 litres malt vinegar
2 tablespoons each curry
powder and flour
1 tablespoon each mustard
powder, ground ginger,
ground cinnamon and
mixed spice
1 teaspoon celery salt
1/3 cup each salt and treacle
6 cups brown sugar

Place fruit, onions and garlic in a large saucepan and cover with 3 litres of vinegar. Bring to the boil, then simmer until fruit and onions are quite tender. Strain through a sieve and return liquid to the pan.

Mix together the rest of the ingredients, stirring in the remaining 1/2 litre of vinegar to make a paste. Pour into the strained liquid. Stir until well blended and boil for 15 minutes.

Pour sauce into preheated clean bottles, holding bottles over the hot pan to retain heat. Seal bottles with a cork or screw-top while sauce is still hot.

Makes 4–5 litres.

Wonton Sauce

It's easy-peasy to make, and just what you need with wontons, samosas and spring rolls.

6 tablespoons apricot jam
3 tablespoons white vinegar
2 tablespoons hot water

Mix ingredients together well in a small bowl.

Serve as a dipping sauce with spring rolls, dim sum and other Asian savouries.

Makes 125ml ($1/2$ cup).

Tamarillo Sauce

High in Vitamin C, high in colour, high in flavour.

4kg tamarillos, peeled and
   chopped coarsely
2 large onions, peeled and
   chopped coarsely
1kg apples, peeled, cored
   and chopped
1kg brown sugar
2 tablespoons each salt and
   ground black pepper
1 tablespoon each ground
   allspice and ground cloves
$3/4$ teaspoon cayenne pepper
600ml malt vinegar

Prepare fruit and place all ingredients in a large saucepan. Bring to the boil, lower the heat and cook gently for 3 hours. Strain and bottle.

Makes about 1.5 litres.

Chillied Sherry (Pili Pili)

An easy way to add chilli flavour to soups and stews. Its hotness depends on the type of chillis used. Tabasco or bird's-eye chillis make it very hot indeed. Some naturopaths recommend adding half a teaspoon of the liquid to your morning pot of tea to ward off arthritis.

handful of hot red chillies
dry sherry

Wash chillies and snip off stalks. Dry them well. Place in a small sterilised jar, standing them up as much as possible. Add sufficient sherry to cover them completely and let stand for a month to allow the chilli flavour to permeate the sherry.

Use in any dish requiring a shot of heat such as soups, stews, curries and dressings — or in a morning cuppa! Start with a few drops and increase the amount according to your tolerance for hot foods.

Salsas & Spreads

Burro Rosso

Make this burro rosso, or red butter, in late summer when red capsicums are at their sweetest. Freeze it for use as a creamy sauce for pasta or with chicken or pork at any time of the year.

2 large red capsicums
2 cloves garlic, chopped
2 tablespoons tomato paste
1 tablespoon fresh basil or
  parsley, chopped
1 teaspoon each ground
  paprika and salt
1/4 cup butter

Grill capsicums in the oven until charred all over. Place in a plastic or brown paper bag for 10 minutes. Pull off charred skin, remove core and seeds, and chop flesh roughly.

Place chopped capsicum, garlic, tomato paste, herbs, paprika and salt in a food processor and blend together until it is a chunky cream. Melt butter and, with the processor running, add to the tomato mixture. Blend just long enough to combine. If not using immediately, spoon into containers and freeze until required.

Makes 1 cup.

Cajun Salsa

2 cucumbers, peeled and
  thinly sliced
1 hardboiled egg, chopped
1 tablespoon cider vinegar
2 tablespoons sour cream
1/2 teaspoon salt
1 hot red chilli, chopped

If cucumber is mature and seeds are tough, discard seeds.

Combine cucumber and egg. Mix together vinegar, sour cream and salt. Pour over the cucumber and egg mixture and fold together. Sprinkle chilli on top, cover and refrigerate for at least 30 minutes to allow the flavours to blend.

Makes enough for 6 servings. Keeps well for 1 week.

Mexican Salsa

This recipe comes from a food writer who lives in Oaxaca, Mexico: it's the real thing.

4 ripe avocados
3 large cloves garlic,
  crushed
2 hot green chillis, seeds
  removed, finely diced
3–4 peaches or pears,
  peeled and diced
1/2 cup seedless grapes,
  halved
2 tablespoons lime juice
1/3 cup pomegranate seeds
sea salt to taste

Remove the skin and stones of avocados. Crush in a mortar with the garlic to make a smooth paste. Add all other ingredients and mix together, adding salt to taste.

Serve with corn tortillas.

Makes about 3 cups. Best used within 3 days.

Apple Salsa

1 each green and red apple,
   skin on, diced
2 tablespoons chopped
   fresh coriander
2 tablespoons fresh lime
   juice
1 tablespoon liquid honey

Mix all ingredients together.

Serve with barbecued pork.

Use immediately.

Nectarine Salsa

Make this when nectarines are in season or when good Californian fruit is cheap. The fresh, light flavours marry well with heavy foods; I particularly like it with roast or grilled lamb. Double the quantities if you are feeding more than 4 people.

1 large nectarine, wiped
   clean and diced
10cm-length telegraph or
   Lebanese cucumber
2 tablespoons diced red
   capsicum
rind and juice of 1 lemon
1/2 small fresh chilli,
   chopped, or a sprinkling of
   piri piri sauce
1 tablespoon chopped fresh
   coriander

Mix all ingredients together, place in a small glass bowl or other attractive serving dish.

Makes 1 cup. Use within 1 day.

Mango Salsa

1 mango, peeled and diced
1/2 red onion, diced small
1 teaspoon grated root
  ginger
1 tablespoon chopped mint
1 red chilli, seeds removed,
  chopped
1 tablespoon lime cordial

Mix all ingredients together and stand for 30 minutes before serving.

Makes 1 cup.

Use within 1 day.

Feijoa Salsa

The mixture of pure vanilla and salt gives this salsa a great flavour, and the blackcurrant and balsamic lend an attractive colour.

10 feijoas
1/2 teaspoon grated root
  ginger
2 tablespoons blackcurrant
  extract
1 tablespoon balsamic
  vinegar
good sprinkle of Equagold
  Vanilla and Herb Sea Salt

Cut feijoas in half and dig out flesh with a teaspoon. Chop flesh and place in a small bowl. Add all other ingredients and mix together well. Serve immediately.

Serve with barbecued, grilled or roast pork or chicken.

Serves 6–8 people. Keeps for 2 days in the refrigerator.

Peach-perfect Salsa

If you like the great combination of chilli and coriander, you'll love this salsa. The flavour is fresh and zingy without being overpowering. A single chilli gives this just the right amount of heat.

1kg peaches, peeled and cut
    into small chunks
1 large red capsicum, cut into
    small dice
1 hot red chilli (jalapeño or
    similar), seeds removed,
    finely chopped
rind and juice of 2 limes
3 tablespoons chopped fresh
    coriander

Prepare peaches, capsicum and chilli and place in a medium-sized bowl. Grate lime rind and squeeze juice (there should be about 1 teaspoon of rind and 2 tablespoons of juice).

Add lime juice, 1 teaspoon of grated rind and the chopped coriander to fruit mixture. Stir together and leave to stand for at least 30 minutes. Leaving the salsa to stand for longer adds to the spicy flavour.

Serve with tortilla chips or seaweed-flavoured rice crackers.

Makes 4–5 cups. Use within 2 days.

Pineapple Salsa

350–400g (2 cups) fresh
  pineapple, diced
2 tablespoons muscovado
  sugar
1 fresh red chilli, finely
  chopped
1 tablespoon sugar
2 spring onions, chopped into
  1cm lengths
1 tablespoon lemon juice
1 tablespoon chopped fresh
  coriander

Mix all ingredients together and pile into a serving dish.
Refrigerate for 4 hours to allow flavours to blend.

Makes 2 cups. Keeps for 4 days in the refrigerator.

Salsa Verde

The name translates to 'green sauce'. Various salsas verde appear in Italian and Spanish cuisine; the following version featuring tomatillos is very Mexican.

300g tomatillos, stem ends
  removed
1 small white onion, peeled
  and finely chopped
2–4 small, very hot chillies
2–4 cloves garlic
1 tablespoon or more
  chopped fresh coriander

Process all ingredients in a food processor.

Makes 2 cups.

Use within 2 days.

Mint and Fruit Salsa

An uncooked, chunky salsa that can double as a chutney. It's truly sensational with chicken curry.

$1/2$ cup raisins

$1/2$ cup dates, stoned and
  chopped

1 packed cup mint leaves

1 medium apple, peeled and
  cored

1 medium red onion, peeled
  and chopped

1 orange, peeled and pith
  removed

2 cups spiced white vinegar

2 tomatoes, skinned and
  chopped

Combine raisins and dates in a blender and process until they are in small dice. Add mint, apple, onion and orange and process until chunky, stopping before it is finely chopped. Stir in spiced vinegar and tomatoes. Pack into jars and seal.

Use with egg, vegetable, pork and chicken dishes.

Makes 2 x 350ml jars.

Roast Garlic and Thyme Paté

Yum! This aromatic paté with a wonderful flavour has a wide range of uses and is a favourite of garlic lovers. Roasting removes the pungent breath that can follow garlic over-indulgence.

400g garlic (about 20 small
    bulbs)
extra virgin olive oil
large bunch of fresh thyme
1 cup Greek or natural
    yoghurt
4 teaspoons sea salt

Preheat oven to 180°C. Cut garlic bulbs in half across the middle. Brush cut edges with olive oil, place in an oven dish and roast for about 45–55 minutes until soft.

Squeeze soft garlic pulp from its outside case. Strip thyme leaves away from stalks. Place thyme leaves and garlic pulp in a mortar and pestle and pound until smooth.

Place garlic and thyme paste in a blender, add yoghurt and salt and purée until smooth.

The paté serves as a spread on focaccia bread or crostini, or as a dip with crisped pita bread, corn chips or crackers. Can also be spread over chicken before baking, to sandwich lamb cutlets together, or to stuff a crown roast.

Makes about 1 cup. Keep refrigerated and use within 1 week.

Basil Pesto

If the price of good Parmesan is too off-putting, Pecorino Romano — an Italian cheese with some of the flavour of Parmigiano Reggiano or Grana Padano — is a fair substitute and much cheaper.

1 packed cup fresh
  basil leaves
1 cup pine nuts
2 fat cloves garlic
1 cup grated Parmesan
  cheese
$1/2$ teaspoon salt
$1/4$–$1/2$ cup extra virgin
  olive oil

Wash basil leaves if necessary. Place basil, pine nuts, garlic and cheese in a blender and whiz until it turns into a thick purée. Add salt and give it another whiz.

With the blender running, gradually pour in the olive oil, a little at a time, checking that each addition is fully blended, until pesto is thick and creamy. If not for immediate use, cover with a little olive oil.

Perfect with pasta but also good on jacket potatoes, added to vegetables soups, spread on toast and bruschetta, and tossed into green salads.

Makes about $1^1/2$ cups.

Sundried Tomato Pesto

150g sundried tomatoes
  in oil
1/2 cup freshly grated
  parmesan cheese
1/2 cup pine nuts
1/2 cup fresh basil leaves
1/2 cup extra virgin olive oil

Blend all ingredients together, including the oil from the tomatoes, until finely chopped. Scoop into a small white bowl.

Serve with melba toast or rice crackers.

Caçik

Yoghurt and cucumber salad or dip comes in many variations in Middle Eastern cookery. In Indian cookery, it goes by the name of raita. In Turkey, it's known as tzatziki.

1 cup plain acidophilus
  yoghurt
2 tablespoons chopped fresh
  mint
2 cloves garlic, finely
  chopped
1 teaspoon each salt and
  sugar
1/2 large or 1 small
  cucumber, peeled and
  coarsely grated

Mix together yoghurt, mint, garlic and seasoning. Just before serving, grate cucumber and add to the dish. Top with a few more chopped mint leaves.

Serve with crisp pita bread or as a side dish with curry.

Eat the day it is made.

Port Wine Cheese

150g tasty or colby cheese,
   grated
50g butter
1 tablespoon port wine
1/2 teaspoon each ground
   nutmeg and ground
   cardamom
1/4 teaspoon ground cloves

Blend all ingredients together and pack into little earthenware jars. Simple!

Makes about 1 cup.

English Potted Cheese

Keep some of this in the refrigerator to serve on toast or crackers with a cool beer or a glass of red wine.

450g tasty cheese, grated
1/2 teaspoon freshly grated
   nutmeg
pinch of cayenne pepper
2 tablespoons dry sherry
1 tablespoon brandy

Place cheese in the blender or electric mixer with nutmeg, cayenne pepper, sherry and brandy. Blend well. Pack into terracotta or glass pots.

Serve with foccacia, toast or crackers.

Makes about 2 cups.

Parmesan Ice cream

What our grandmothers knew as potted cheese now turns up on café menus as Parmesan Ice cream. Whatever it's called, it's a delicious spread.

150g Parmesan cheese, shredded
1 tablespoon flour
1/2 teaspoon freshly grated nutmeg
pinch of cayenne pepper
100ml cream
2 tablespoons dry sherry
1 teaspoon French mustard

Toss the cheese in flour, nutmeg and cayenne pepper.

Heat the cream to just under boiling point, add the cheese mix and stir until cheese is melted and blended. Add sherry and mustard, and stir until blended. Remove from heat immediately, pour into a bowl and chill until required. Surprisingly, it will set solid.

Serve with bread sticks, wheat crackers or toast triangles.

Makes about 1 cup.

Salsas & Spreads

Tapenade

This is a variation of the classic Mediterranean tapenade — this version is without the anchovies.

1 cup black olives, pitted

2 teaspoons capers

1 clove garlic, crushed

1 tablespoon extra virgin
  olive oil

1 teaspoon finely chopped
  parsley

4 tablespoons sour cream

Combine all ingredients in a blender until well mixed. Store in the refrigerator and allow to stand for 10 minutes at room temperature before use.

Makes 1 cup.

Sweet Treats

Candied Cherry Tomatoes

A Greek friend told me his grandmother used to preserve tomatoes to serve as a sweet-meat. I used coffee sugar crystals, which give a wonderful golden colour and full flavour to the syrup.

500g ripe cherry tomatoes
2 cups coffee sugar crystals
2 cups cold water
2 cinnamon sticks
thin strips of lemon rind

Cut around the core end of each tomato. This allows the skins to be easily removed after cooking.

Bring sugar crystals and water to the boil, stirring carefully as the sugar dissolves to ensure it does not burn. Add cinnamon stick and lemon rind, and keep at boiling point for 5 minutes.

Add tomatoes, bring sugar syrup back to the boil and simmer for a few minutes until skins detach. Remove whole tomatoes with a slotted spoon and discard skins. Place tomatoes in hot sterilised jar and top with syrup.

Serve on a teaspoon with tea, coffee or a sweet wine.

Makes 2 small jars.

Candied Peel

The first time I candied peel in this way, I ended up with citrus toffee. It was delicious but not what I wanted! The trick is to keep the heat low and remove the saucepan from the heat before the liquid has completely evaporated.

4 oranges, grapefruit or
   large lemons (or a
   combination of these)
cold water
2 cups sugar
1 cup water
4 tablespoons caster sugar

Using a potato peeler, peel citrus fruit thinly (avoid cutting into the pith). Cut peel into strips about 5cm wide (the wider the strips, the easier they will be to handle). Place in a saucepan, cover with cold water and bring to the boil. Lower the heat and simmer for 20 minutes.

In another pan, combine sugar and water. Bring to the boil gently, stirring occasionally, until sugar has dissolved. Remove from the heat.

Drain peel and add to sugar syrup. Over a low heat, bring to the boil, then turn the heat as low as possible to keep syrup simmering gently for 1 hour or until liquid has almost evaporated. Using tongs, lift peel out of syrup and place on a tray lined with baking paper. Set in a cool place for 2 days to dry. Toss in caster sugar and store in an airtight container.

Chocolate-coated Orange Peel

Prepare candied peel as opposite. Melt some chocolate or couverture in a saucepan over hot water. Dip each strip of peel, lay on baking paper and leave to set. Yum!

Dried Citrus Peel

More From the Cook's Garden authors Mary Browne, Helen Leach and Nancy Tichborne recommend drying citrus skins that would otherwise be discarded.

Pare peel off fruit, lay it in a dehydrator and follow appliance instructions.

Use for grating in place of fresh peel.

Cherry Preserves

Whole cherries cooked in heavy syrup are wonderful on their own, with a dollop of cream as a dessert, added to fruit or spread between layers of chocolate sponge to make the notoriously rich black forest cherry cake.

500g white sugar
2 cups water
500g red or black cherries,
   unstoned

Heat 225g (1 cup) of sugar with water and boil for 5 minutes. Add cherries and cook for 15–20 minutes until tender. Add remaining sugar and cook rapidly until it begins to thicken. Skim if necessary. Pour into hot sterilised jars and seal.

Makes about 1 litre.

Preserved Ginger

Green or root ginger usually lasts well when stored in a cool place. It tends to go soft when stored in the freezer, although the flavour is still good. When you're using ginger in stews and dressings, preserving it in sherry is a wise move.

fresh root ginger
dry sherry

Break apart sections of ginger and cut into 10cm lengths. Scrap skin off each piece. Place ginger pieces in a clean jar and add enough sherry to cover. Screw the cap on tightly.

Use ginger as desired. The ginger-flavoured sherry can be used in soups, ice creams and desserts.

Quince Paste

Membrillo, or quince paste, is a popular sweetmeat in Mediterranean countries. This method is adapted from one of classical food writer Elizabeth David's recipes.

2kg quinces
about 1.5kg sugar

Wipe quinces clean and steam whole in a pressure cooker for 25 minutes. When cool enough to handle, quarter quinces, remove cores and any discoloured skin.

Cut into chunks and weigh. Blend in a food processor until reasonably smooth. Pour into a preserving pan. Add an equal weight of sugar and bring to the boil. Boil well, stirring as often as possible, until mixture begins to leave the sides of the pan. It will have darkened to a rich reddish brown colour (this took $1^1/_2$ hours on a humid March day in Auckland).

Remove from heat and ladle into sponge roll tins. Smooth top with a spatula. Leave to cool.

Place in an oven set at the lowest temperature (a warming oven is ideal) and leave for several hours. It should now be a firm paste that can be cut into pieces with a knife. Store in an airtight container.

Serve the Spanish way with a slice of soft white cheese and a few good almonds or walnuts. It is very sweet, but delicious.

Prunes in Port

A superb addition to the store cupboard. When a quick but impressive dessert is required, simply pour the prunes into attractive glass or china bowls with a dollop of cream, crème fraîche or ice-cream.

500g prunes
1¹/₂ cups port wine
¹/₂ cup sugar
rind from 1 orange, cut in
   fine strips
6 cloves
1 cinnamon stick

Prick prunes with a needle. Bring port to the boil with sugar, orange rind, cloves and cinnamon stick. Allow to simmer for 5 minutes.

Ladle prunes into hot clean jars and top up with port, adding more if necessary to fill the jars.

Makes 2 x 500ml jars.

Prunes in Gin

These are even more simple to make than Prunes in Port. Be warned: they pack a punch after they've been soaking for a few months.

250g prunes • ¹/₃ cup sugar • 1 or more cups gin

Place prunes in clean jars. Sprinkle sugar over and top with gin. Leave for at least 2 months before using.

Candied Ginger in Syrup, see page 120, Spiced Rhubarb Conserve, see page 66, and Prunes in Port

Candied Ginger in Syrup

Remember when preserved ginger was available in attractive blue and white china jars, and the ginger was immersed in a delicious sticky syrup? This recipe is the nearest I've come to recreating that childhood treat. Buy good quality root ginger that looks fresh; I tried making this with the ginger plant that flourishes in Auckland, and the result was stringy and inedible.

250g fresh root ginger
1 cup water
1¹/₂ cups sugar

Scrub ginger to remove its fine brown skin. Chop into pieces about 5cm square. Place in a saucepan and cover with water. Bring to the boil and simmer for 15 minutes. Test for tenderness.

Reserve 1 cup of the cooking water and add it to the sugar in a separate pan. Bring to the boil and simmer for 5 minutes. Add diced ginger and simmer for 45–60 minutes or until soft and sticky. Spoon ginger into sterilised jars and cover with boiling syrup. Seal.

Makes 2 x 250ml jars.

Brandied Fruits

Also known as Tutti Frutti. Substitute rum for brandy and it becomes Rum Pot.

3 cups ripe strawberries or
   ripe stone fruit
3 cups sugar
3 cups good brandy

Wipe strawberries carefully and place in an earthenware jar with a close-fitting lid. If using other fruit, stone and cut into chunks. Sprinkle sugar over fruit, then gently add the brandy.

Leave for a month before using. As fruit is used, more can be added, topping up the brandy if necessary.

Makes a great sauce for ice-cream or other desserts.

Fruit Leather

2kg apricots, peaches or
   apples
1kg sugar

Wipe fruit clean and steam whole until they begin to soften. Allow to cool enough to handle. Quarter fruits, remove cores and any discoloured skin. Cut into chunks. Blend in a food processor until reasonably smooth.

Pour into a preserving pan or saucepan with a wide mouth. Add sugar and bring to the boil. Boil well, stirring as often as possible, until mixture begins to leave the sides of the pan. Remove from heat.

Lay baking paper on an oven tray and spread fruit on this to a depth of 2–3cm. Smooth over the top with a spatula and place in an oven at the lowest temperature (100C°) for at least 10 hours. It will be dry to touch when it is ready. It can also be dried in a dehydrator, or even outside if the sun is strong enough.

Cut into strips, wrap in plastic food wrap and store in an airtight container.

Serve with creamy cheeses, use to stuff a pork loin or add it to a packed lunch when you're on a long walk.

Glossary

Chutneys: Chutneys are made from fruit, vegetables and vinegar cooked together slowly to form a soft, thick pulp. Flavours are blended together and individual chunks of fruit or vegetable may no longer be recognisable. Chutneys are seldom eaten on their own: they can accompany a main meal or be spread on toast or crackers.

Conserves: A conserve is usually a rich jam containing chunks of whole fruit suspended in thick syrup. Some conserves can be eaten with a spoon as a sweet treat.

Jams and Jellies: Jams are made from fruit and sugar boiled together. The name is presumed to come from the fruit being crushed, or jammed, together to produce a pulp. Jellies are made from the strained juice produced when fruit is simmered slowly, as for jams. Jellies in particular flourish when made in small quantities.

Pickles: Often pickles comprise just one type of fruit or vegetable, cooked and stored in a spiced vinegar solution. The vegetables remain individually identifiable. Some vegetables stay crisp, and so can be used as a winter salad. Pickles are usually ready for use in 1 month.

Relish: Relish is an all-embracing term used for a side dish or accompaniment ready for immediate eating.

Salsas: Salsa is the Spanish word for 'sauce'. In Spain the sauce is usually an integral part of the dish instead of a separate component. The word is now used to describe an assembly of fresh ingredients that add pizzazz to other foods. Some salsas are simply uncooked chutneys.

Sauces: Sauces consist of ingredients cooked together to give a consistency that can be poured. They are usually left to mellow for a month before eating.

Index

ACKNOWLEDGEMENTS

Special thanks to all the friends who provided recipes, ideas, support, encouragement, and of course jars – including Caryl Bottomley, Rosemary Jane Calver, Heather Clendon, Mary Hunter, Dot Lamb, Fay Mason, Suzanne Murrell, Alison Roberton, Anna Tucker and Junette Wrathall.

Food and travel are the big passions in Jill Brewis' life. Fortunately her current role as president of the New Zealand Guild of Food Writers keeps her involved with many interesting 'foodie' issues and her love of travel is regularly indulged through her visits to family, including seven grandchildren, who are spread over three continents.

Jill has many years' experience as a freelance writer, food writer and editor in New Zealand and abroad. She is the author of *Parnell Pot Pourri, Colonial Fare, Home Landscape Design for New Zealanders, Muffin Time*, and the compiler of *The Dessert Cookbook* and *The Essential Digby Law*.